#EVENTPROOF

by

Tanzania T Rice

Table of Contents

1   Event Control

2   Micro-Manage (Page 12)

3   WORK HARD (Page 17)

4 Personally (Page 24)

5 The Blueprint (Page 28)

6   #Eventproof? (Page 33)

PART II

7 The Marketing Bean (Page 47)

9   The Tech Bean (Page 61)

Conclusion (Page 64)

Introduction

This two-part development book was created with the passion and dedication of my major purpose in life. I know that I was created to create life-changing moments, I just used to be so unaware of how to tap into that. I wanted to produce a guide for women and men that have the skill, however, want to enhance and develop it. I was a college junior working at my first restaurant job. I was making BIG tips; coming home with at least two to three hundred a night. I would go to the bank and deposit all my cash, and the bank teller would look at me with an odd face. No, no stripper, just a college student, with a hospitality major that's trying to get it the right way. It was the first time I had ever created a family work environment. I had a best friend named, Nate, and to this day, Nate and I are still in contact. The restaurant was known for being the busiest in the town during the weekend evenings. That's when most of the servers, including myself because I would school during the week, would be working. Before every shift, Nate would make me come to the back, while he smoked his God-forsaken cigarette, pray over the shift. His prayers used to touch my soul, while when it was my turn, I felt like my prayer was weak. However, I stuck with him, crafting better prayers and even starting to pray throughout the day by myself. This is not to say that I was not religious. I attended church and was even on the dance team at church; however, I could never really tap into expressions my spirituality. One day, I watched my manager, Miguel, hand Nate a book. Nate stated to me, "Hey, you ever read this book called "The Secret"?" insistently shook my head no. When I was younger, I loved reading novels. But lately, the only books I was picking up was the ones my professors were making me pay hundreds of dollars for. He suggested that I read the book, for it would assist in my spiritual journey. Overlooking and ignoring him, I moved on with life. It wasn't until I started watching the changes that were happening to nate and how it seemed as though, mentally, he seemed stronger. I decided to read the book. (Yes, this all started with that crazy famous book "The Secret," but it's more, just wait.) My best friend, Jasmine and I, started reading the book together. We even formed a book club from the book. One thing that I have always been was curious, I swear I should have been a detective, but then I think about the danger, and I couldn't even see myself! I've always taken that extra step to answer the why. As I read "The Secret" I always wondered, where is she getting this information from? Why is she getting this information? Where did she get it from, and who did they get it from? My best friend and I, started researching the individuals that she was quoting in the book and looking in the back at the glossary. We started researching those authors and reading some of their books. It took us on an amazing spiritual journey that has brought me to where I am now. Before reading "The Secret," I was going about life, not really sure what my major purpose in life was. During my ""The Secret" investigation," I discovered Napoleon Hill. An amazing author and speaker on the development of the mind and marketing. He's the one that the source always led back to. I started reading more and more books from Mr. Hill, listening to his speeches, books on tapes and even reading books from people that were writing books from him. I sat down one day, by Mr. Hill instructions, and wrote out my major purpose in life on a piece of paper and posted it on my wall, right beside the door. So that whenever I left out the door, I would always see it. I created a vision board, with photos and quotes of people and things I aspired to have. Day by day, month by month and year by year I am succeeding exactly what I've created on that paper. I used to be embarrassed to show this to people, but I tell this to people now so that they can have a better understanding of how important writing out exactly what you want matters. You have to excuse the grammar, etc, I just was going off my mind. My major purpose in life read like this:

"I will become a celebrity event planner with my own Fortune 500 Company. I will find a mentor that will guide me to be exactly where I want to be. I will become an event planner to the stars. Actors, music artists, fashion and more. I will work hard, and smart. I will be at the right place at the right time, always. I will reward my mentor with funds and praise. I believe in myself. I believe in my family and friends for support. I believe in those who work with me. I believe in my employer, that I will soon be my own employer. I believe that God will lend me everything I need with which to succeed if I do my best to earn it through faithful and honest service."

The end was a little help from napoleon hill, haha, but that is the mission that I read before I left the house every day. And before I went to sleep at night. As time went on things were manifesting before my eyes. I got a text about a radio station that was looking for interns. I immediately hopped on it. I ended up working for a

National DJ that was heavily in the music business. I started working for the radio station and learning my craft while also meeting some awesome people. I was a photographer, graphic designer, videographer, personality, event planner, marketer and more. Unaware that I was forming into a Fortune 500 CEO. I was 22 when I was told about a seminar about how to write a book. By this time, I had planned events with TV One, Cassidy, Red Cafe, seminars and more! I was getting better and better with each event. Forming myself into exactly who I wanted to be. A celebrity event planner with her own fortune 500 company.

What stuck to me most about Napoleon Hill, was this one book called, "Think and Grow Rich." The chapters were all ways to increase your marketing tactics; however, the approach was more mental. It opened my eyes to marketing and branding myself, and understanding that marketing is more than "by-the-book" methods, it's your mental attitude. Some still think that marketing is about numbers, and sometimes it is when it's time to do the SWOT analysis. However, when beginning a brand the fundamentals, having a positive mental attitude, pleasing personality, master alliance and more. It was not until I learn these fundamentals, did I successfully build myself and my brand. I used the 10 secrets of success from Napoleon Hill and crafted it into an event planners and entrepreneur ultimate guide. Not only are they relatable, however, but I also cover each standpoint, with examples and views from the events world. Something that is much more cut-throat and fast-paced. It's important when approaching this world that you are given all the mental and physical tools to succeed to your best ability.

Nowadays, event planners are known for running around with the walkie-talkies like a chicken with his head cut off! Yes, some moments can get a little crazy. However, you may see some event planners that are poised and filled with complete serenity. That is the event planner that this book will build you up to be. Becoming a successful event planner means standing in your craft with confidence. To be able to do that you have to know and understand the fundamentals of being #EventProof. You'll need to highlight some things, stop and reevaluate some things and more with this book. The most important part is you will not only be able to build a successful event company. However, you will become a successful event planner!

Think the most amazing thing about being an event planner is that, with all the hats that we wear, we create the ultimate branding paradise. Events are the number one marketing tool for an event company. They hold such significant, memorable moments that allows you to treasure the brand even more. Use that power to your complete advantage. Event planners hold so much power within all the industries. Whether it is medicine, music, arts, science and more. Every industry is craving for a gathering to expand the future of generations to come. We are given a huge responsibility to the people. We must create unforgettable memories. I know that this book will establish a groundbreaking change in your craft. Using these fundamental things have changed my life drastically. I owe all my success to these chapters. I wish you all the success on your journey. Upon completion of all the chapters in this book, consider yourself, #Eventproof!

Chapter 1 – Having Self-Control

Autumn was coming to an end. All the insects and animals were working very hard to stock their larders with enough food to last them the winter. They all knew that winter time would be tough – it would be cold and food would be scarce. As it would get dark really soon, it would be difficult to go looking for food. Therefore, everyone was working hard, all except Mr. Grasshopper. He loved autumn. Autumn was a time when the leaves change color. It was all so pretty. The trees seemed to be on fire with red, yellow and orange leaves, which then fell off and covered the ground. There was a pleasant breeze too. Mr. Grasshopper spent his days playing. He jumped from leaf to leaf and from one fallen twig to another. What he liked best was the way the leaves bounced when he jumped off them, and how the leaf he landed on swayed with his weight. Life is lovely, the world is beautiful, and I want to play forever…‖ he sang.

Just then little Miss Ant happened to pass by. She was dragging a heavy grain of rice behind her. —Oowf. This is so heavy. I wish I could get some help with this. I should have asked my brother to come along to help me,‖ she was muttering. —Oh, do you need help?‖ asked Mr. Grasshopper. —Yes, sir. Would you give me a hand? My ant hill is just a few trees away, but this is so heavy,‖ replied the ant happily —Naw! First, you come and play with me for some time, then I shall gladly help you. What are you toiling for anyway? Autumn is so beautiful; you too should enjoy the weather while you can,‖ the grasshopper said. —No, Mr. Grasshopper. You too must start collecting your food for the winter. Otherwise, it will be tough as there won't be anything to eat,‖ said the concerned ant. —Nothing doing. I will go out and find all the food I want when I am hungry. Right now it is time to play and have a party,‖ the silly grasshopper replied. So Miss Ant just shook her head and went on – —Huff, puff, huff, puff.‖ Then winter came. It was so cold that the ants didn't dare to come out. But their tummies were full, and they were warm and happy. Actually, everyone was warm and happy, except for Mr. Grasshopper. He was cold and hungry. As he went hunting for food only when it was less cold than usual, he got very little to eat and soon became weak with hunger. —Oh, why did I spend my days playing? I should have listened to the ant...‖ he thought with regret.

"Here are some of the more common ways we lose self-control: we set no goals or impossible goals; we lose control or don't pay attention to our goals or our behavior; we quit because we get tired or stressed and weakened; we attend to our immediate situation and needs overlooking long-range goals; we misjudge what is important to do; we focus on calming our emotions but neglect doing our tasks or solving our problems; we become obsessed with protecting our egos and neglect getting the job done; we let the initial failure lead to a "snowballing" of many failures, we believe in venting our feelings rather than in eliminating the emotions; we decide we are helpless or bad and stop trying in order to avoid further failure."-

Event planning is one of the most important fields to have a steady foundation. Ants grow their foundation through many months. Many know insects as creatures that are very team orientated. But one interesting thing that I see about insects is that they all still enforce the knowledge. No matter who may know what already, they make sure that they know for themselves, and that themselves and their families are protected. We can learn such amazing things from creatures about self-control. I say as an event planner we have to be all the animals in the kingdom. We have to be the cheetah, moving quick and fast. We have to be the snake, aware of our surroundings. We have to be the monkey, the genius. We wear all hats, and for that, your self-control has to be controlled at all times.

Setting Goals: Nothing is more important than assuring you know where you're going. Setting "doable" and unrealistic goals are the first on the list of any successful event planner. A list of goals should be the start of your day, events, meeting and more. Being as detailed as possible in your list is the most important. Don't overlook anything. I say, doable because those are the goals that you KNOW that you can get accomplished because you have the necessary tools to execute. Don't think you'll remember something. Treat your mind like a dummy. The most important thing to do is write down every detail of the event that must be executed. Which breaks down into categories depending on your initial responsibility for the event. That is management, decor, food & beverage and logistics. Then generate each into a timeline. Once you've got your timeline, properly assign jobs. Each job should have set goals, which will in the end result be making the ultimate goal a success. Breaking down, analyzing, your to-do list one by one is important each day. Also bring your team together when creating the goals, this makes sure you don't miss everything. Create a brainstorming environment. Research good brainstorming games. That way the creative things that you all come up with, you have a list of how it will be accomplished. Use your bullet points to be the platform of your activity and outline that platform and execute them. This will help you dissect details. Something that we will discuss in great detail in this book. If I had a million dollars for every time, I say "detail" in this book I would be rich. Keeping track of your goals is the next important thing. Matter of fact that should be on your to-do list. Evaluation days of your goals. Every detail! Don't overlook anything.

Managing Your Behavior: With a plan like yours, it's no doubt that it will succeed IF you don't allow anything or anyone to take you off your course. Remember that all tests come in the funniest situations at the funniest times. Anyone with sufficient goals and plans to execute them is destined to go where they imagine. Make sure you do your research as much as possible for all elements of the event. Knowledge and Power can conquer all. So yes, the vendor might show up late, but you've got a second plan handy for that. The easiest way to control your behavior is to remain a positive mental attitude as much as possible. When thinking positive your mind is clear and ready and open to ideas and suggestions. Many people lack listening skills when their behavior is under managed. I want to tell you a story, and I want you to reflect on this. I was a part of the coordinating team of my first big showcase with a woman movie producer for HBO and VH1. I was working at the radio station, and I had a few events up my sleeve by that time. I had attended numerous showcases, so seeing them being executed correctly and incorrectly was quickly noted. We were working with another radio station for this event from Philadelphia, and we allowed them to take over the organization and hosting, and we would just take charge of the promotion. Everything went horrible, the sound was not working, the judges had poor material to use to keep up with their voting, and the artists were heated! The ladies whose event it was, VH1, was livid.

I've always been known to have the most positive attitude in the room, so she immediately told me to take control. The lady that was in charge of all this mess, the Philly station owner, heard that I was directed to take charge and she went wild. Yelled at me and told me she wanted me to get out VIP. Started yelling at the artist, just being very emotional. She was looked at in disgusts from every angle of the room. How dare she get upset because her organization is actually not organized at all. Then why get mad at me? I'm clearly an event planner, and she was a station owner/host. She doesn't know a thing about running a successful event. At least that's what her uncontrollable behavior portrayed. You see how easily uncontrollable behavior can expose your flaws? Maybe misunderstood flaws. Now I could have helped organize it better, got the crowd hype while they were fixing the sound. Gave her tips on how to better organize the artists. However, after her approach to me, I let melt! I quietly walked around to every artist and apologized from my station for the experience. The second time we had the showcase, I was in full charge of the showcase. From organizing and execution. She sat there quietly, like a mouse in the corner.

That brings me to the next important thing! Be aware! Self-control has a lot to do with being aware of your surroundings. Always understand your clients and the audience. Who's in the audience, where are they from? What do they like to hear? As I said as event planners, we wear all hats. Get you a good five or seven books dealing with psychology and sociology. Those were my two favorite subjects in college. They teach you how to make the event FEEL real. Self-control is making the other person feel. However, before analyzing anyone else, you must analyze yourself! Go to a few people you've known for a while and begin asking them about your characteristics. And tell them don't be afraid, spill the beans. Be strong; they're just words. I suffered from being sensitive for such a long time; I still have that issue sometimes, I have to be transparent.

It ended friendships, relationships, and a lot of missed opportunities.

Once I overcame my pride, I started to take criticism better. But it all

happened for a reason. When I finally took into the realization of

being more aware of my characteristics I started to gain better

relations with like-minded people. Doors were opening, and I was

finally being recognized for what I was born to do. Always make

sure you are beaming. Stay aware of your past, current, and future

moves. Analyze the time spent, people still there and the ones that

are not. Go back to your goals and make sure they are still on the

right path. Details!

If things are not going right, then you must haven't done the right

research. Your self-control is mastered through, what I like to call,

your width and height of knowledge. However, what's a whole

bunch of knowledge that's false worth? I probably change my

channel only when the company is at my house. But I keep the TV

on History Channels when I even get the chance to watch it. I don't

move it because I call it my cheat sheet to facts. You'll be surprised

the correlation of history has on events. Allow your events to MEAN

more, through the feelings of real history. But that's a whole 'other

book that I will write for you soon! But I say that to say, Do research

as much research as you can. I always look up four to five different

ways to do whatever I'm researching at the time before I give in. I

always compare vendors, designs, days, times and anything you can

think I will double check if that is preferable. Now you will not

always be right. There's always someone smarter, and there's always

someone dumber, but no one can use the knowledge you have like

you can. That's a big secret.

Consistency! Consistency! Consistency! I was doing an event one

night. I was a photographer like I said we wear all hats, and it was the biggest Christmas toy drive party of the year. The who's of who's was in the building. I was dressed down! Jeans, no make-up, tennis shoes and an all-white t-Shirt. My mind was set on doing interviews. I was not dressed beautifully, no make-up, I was seriously chilling. The personality that was doing the interviews that night walked up to me and said, "Hey we're about to interview DJ Quick Silva." I was hyped, he's the biggest DJ in the area! However, we are all hardworking in this industry, so I was more so excited about what he had to say. The interview went great, as Tiffany, the personality, wrapped the interview up she asked one great question,"What's something you would say to someone trying to get out in this industry and succeed?" He stated,"Hard work, consistency, and passion." That's it! It stuck to me, and I never forgot his words of wisdom. To this day I live in that body of words. But consistency! Consistency! Consistency! That's so important, you have to remain strong, and you can't quit." People, you have to remain on the path with patterns so strict. You will have to work on weekends. You will have to work on holidays. You will have to execute a meeting or an

event on mommy's birthday. You will have to give up boo loving

time to make sure X, Y, and Z is executed to perfection. No lacking

or slacking, everything has to be consistent. That self-control

requires a separation of emotions and career growth.

Now combine all that with a positive mental attitude, are you set?

When I first turned 22, I got a tattoo on my wrist that stated PMA,

"Positive Mental Attitude." When I say I was stripped of everything,

all my blessings was being taken left and right I was going through

it! I couldn't understand what was going on. I was rushed to the

hospital, and as soon as I was released, I was laid off from my job

the next day. I was being dumped by a dumb boyfriend, and friends

were terrible. I had just got my own apartment, and my roommate

situation was going down the drain! I couldn't understand why I was

going through so much?! Then it hit me; I never once looked down at my wrist when going through any of this. When you implement

things in your life, you have to go by it. If not, you'll do something

called confuse the mind. When you put permanent thoughts into

your subconscious mind, things around will test you. It will test your

new knowledge. NASA probably does the most tests in the world

before even getting close to space. They spend years testing! You

have to stand the test! You cannot call yourself an event planner and

complain at every challenge that comes to you. Cry when things get

hard or quit. Use the tools that you have set up for yourself, in the

beginning, to be successful through the whole journey.

Chapter 2 Micro Manage

Micromanaging is key. Learning how to use all your players wisely. It's important that we understand ourselves and limitations that some circumstances will put us in. Once you've established that solid list tries to stick to it in every aspect of the event that you will encounter. Clients love perfected consistency. Reason being that you would keep the template so distributing tasks will be easier and manageable. Developing a sufficient team is key in and any every aspect of your life. No point in killing yourself. Having a master alliance is way better than having your one positive minds. The collective positive energy of success will flourish through the teamwork. I did not start to flourish into my career until I met my true master alliance – Megan. Who is now, my business partner. Collectively we create amazing experiences! I couldn't be any more proud of us!

Describing the job is a key factor that I think tends to be overlooked at now in this industry. I feel as though just as any normal job - because this is a job of the elite honey – full communication of what is expected from initial HIRING should be discussed. Getting a clear background of their past events and tasks they've worked on. This can be done so easily with two formal interviews and one on the day experience. I believe that this hiring process should be much more intense. The CIA hires 13% 1,700 people that apply. And the hiring process is not easy. They interview your family; I think there are multiple tests. That's what this field should entitle. Family and friends know you best. If that person's own family has not allowed them to plan an event for them or at least coordinate one, they are not to be trusted. Unless you have a case where it's family issues.

But you get the point. I hope. Really ask as many questions as possible. Have 3 people in the room or 3 separate people interview the prospect. Your questions should reflect directly what they would be working on and other departments as well. You want to assure that they are well-rounded. Using a job description template to create your interview questions would be a tremendous help.

So once you've dissected all the beautiful roses and the dead ones, now it's time for quick execution. I have to many times seen a person with total excitement in the interview process, then once on the task, all that was talked about isn't being seen. I am a woman of chances, but I don't do many. 9 is my favorite number, but 3 is at my patience! Watch how the individual uses their time in a day. Most event planners have planners or tablets, or some tool to make us successful on a daily. I do not speak a word my first two weeks to who I hire, but I'm just harsh! So I'll give you the cleaned up version. Depending on who you hire, work with them. Some individuals work differently. Critic their weaknesses, and it will allow their strengths to show. And that is what you need to use to your advantage. The strengths will allow you to know who to place where on the field.

Technology is so amazing. Attend as many webinars, seminars, and conferences that you can to keep yourself up to date on the technology that we can use to manage our companies. Monitoring your employees is 70% of the company, hell 80%! Because you might have employees monitoring the money. Working for a million, maybe billion, dollar hotel Management Company has made me realize that millions can disappear. Because I am writing this book for the millions, so you have to think like that. Watch your dreams and watch your finances. They are two separate things. There are so many apps and systems that you should use and download when first entering into the world of being #Eventproof.

Google drive is first and foremost. Probably one of the easiest ways to maintain synced documents, pictures, meetings, appointments, calendars, and more! Not to mention emails! Google drive is the way to go for a great fresh start with a nice attractive email. Google shows organization and an overall great brand representation. It's an easy productivity software that asks what you've done for the day (via email) and automatically assembles each team member's response in a daily digest to your email. So simple and allows you more free time. Harvest is a great way to track billable hours and easily create invoices for clients. So simple! So the great things about this is that it saves you money and time. Your employee's timesheets are on here, and you also see which client is getting billed for what because it's all tracked. You can still review their work at a time that is convenient for you. Something similar to this that's great is PayPal. I'm sure we have all heard it before however, I am very old-fashioned tech girl that thinks that PayPal has been great over the years. It sends invoices, has bank cards, tracks payments, and collects client's information. The others you can research on your own. I have a whole book to write honey. And more!

Next, you gotta make sure you're taking care of your people. Wages are not enough, but make sure you're not stingy their either. Learn that the more you give, the more you will be given in return. Read that sentence again. Take your staff on luncheons, and have one on ones with them frequently. Make raffles, do giveaways, and make atmosphere fun. Make sure you ask questions and listen. Get to know them and seem to grow a slight interest in their hobbies and lifestyles. Allow them to trust in you, but never draw the line of business and the sincerity of it. Friendships should never be developed and should I not mention you should not even hire them if they are a friend. But I would hope you have good enough sense to know what friends are hirable and friable.

Awards show that you pay attention and gives an incentive of longevity. Titles and awards mean something to people. The more important you look and sound the higher up you are. I guess, but in this field, it's the work you put in. I don't know many award-winning event planners, but that's because I'm not looking. I'm looking for the event execs that have track records of multimillion dollar clients. Those are the ones that have worked skillfully in this industry. They deserve all the money because I was never able to cash a trophy in.

Lastly, make sure you have analyzed and given the employee's amazing critiques. Daily, weekly, monthly and annually. But make sure you are speaking in a monotone, with an unbiased opinion, and caring attitude for the perfection of their workmanship. Assure that it is all documented and both parties have them. Always make sure you have every outlet available to receive comments and concerns from their standpoint. Placement of roles becomes effortless after this has to be given a successful permanent system. Sometimes people are not going to work out, your quickness of assessing will qualify your unattainability in this game. Your team is your core, and they are your true representation. Your reputation is everything! Feelings may be hurt but allowing yourself to be less stressed because you have placed successful management in the business is worth so much more.

Chapter 3 – WORK HARD

With all the fun that's surrounded this is not for the easily distracted. This is for the serious individual that take their craft seriously and above all keep separate the two. Wiz Khalifa, who by the way is one of my favorite rappers, has a song called, Work Hard, Play Hard. That's the same in this field. The perks are amazing, however, only for the deserving. You have to push yourself to that last piece of strength that you have. And then push even harder. Then you can fall out. Then get right back up 2, yes two, minutes later and go hard again. Diddy once said - he's one of my mentors - that you have to hustle till it's only one more second left every single time. Don't hustle like you got tomorrow, grind till you only got one second left every single time! Using all your characteristics and heart and soul in every single event. Never overlook anything, always checking for yourself, team, attendees and most importantly the client. Self-reflection is very important at this point because you cannot break. A lot is dependent on you, and this task will be held as an everlasting moment. Anything with joy has a 70% of being memorized more than a bad memory. You want to be a part of that everlasting memory that changes that person's life. When working your best and giving it you're all the respect you receive from all angles of the event is remarkable. Not to mention how proud of yourself you will be. After every event document what you do though. Try to have a journal where you can free your mind sometimes and learn how to gain complete control of your mind at all times.

I think the Airbnb story of true hard work, dedication, creativity, and patience is shown here. Airbnb is a website that is nationally known for individuals renting their own homes out for amazing prices. I'll wait for them to cut the check to continue giving you all the details. So anyways, the owners were starting the company summer of 2008, and they needed a way to raise money. So they bought a ton of cereal and designed special edition election-themed boxes, released that fall—Obama O's and Cap'n McCain's, which they sold at convention parties for $40 a box. They sold 500 boxes of each cereal, helping them to raise around $30k for Air bnd & Breakfast, what Air Bnb was called at that time. So if anyone knows that whole process itself is work. Now, with all that money the business still did not budge. The site still did not gain much traction initially, and the founders resorted to living off of leftovers of the Cap'n McCain's of because of course the Obama O's sold out! They were at a time they refer to as a real "low point." This low point did not last for long, however, as the following spring, they had dinner with Paul Graham. Air bnd & Breakfast soon joined Y Combinator's 2009 winter class, receiving another $20,000 in funding. They renamed the business Airbnb, and soon received another $600k! Not all events are made for the money. Some are transactions are sent to be of much more meaning. Bigger destinations. A way to gain your network. Giving away free things is the golden apple on the tree of wealth. Give that juicy thing away..for FREE! Your service and product is a blessing. We create it with all our hearts and soul, why not let someone feel special. NOTHING is free nowadays. Go do your research. So imagine the value they will place on what you give them for free.

The delinquency of sponsorships is probably a whole other book. I'll give you the mindset that you should have to create a successful process. Let's start with knowing and fully understanding the event. The knowledge will help you better analyze the brands you will seek after. The event must be studied and given a firm foundation before even going after these sponsors. Knowing what your event truly will offer is the start of your outline. SD: The client must have a well-established brand and idea before coming to you. Set up consulting fees and contracts will help minimize a lot of time wasted. Being the face of the event to secure sponsorships makes our roles so much more interesting. They are true testers of what this field is really involved in which is partially sales. Pretty much the direct field to give you all the business skills training 101. Aren't we lucky! Paying attention to detail at this point is crucial. I can give you a time that I was being so impatient with receiving my success, that I started to put my frustration out on my peers. I would snap on my teammates and the interns that we had at the time. Which was puzzling me because I never used to carry such energy on me. Snapping into it made me realize that, that was holding up my success with landing sponsorships. I would rush through documents, very important detail orientated documents that I thought I knew was good. Taking advantage of the people and opportunities that were in front of me. I learned an amazing lesson, and I ask that you live vicariously through me when I say to take your time and build that foundation of excellence, before asking for people's "hard" earned money for your future magical experience.

As I said, nothing is more important than DETAILS! Details should be a feeling, so it's everlasting in all your thoughts, which soon turns into your actions. Have a positive outlook on details of events. How you develop your mind to see tasks will in the end results. Ladies, and gentlemen, when you are seeking your new relationship fling or what not you pay so much close attention to everything. You first gather yourself and self-evaluate, make sure you are prepared to be in a relationship. I hope, but I know we all don't but we should! After you look into what you would want the prospect inner values and feelings to be like. How you would want them to treat you, speak to you, and overall relate. After we've analyzed what we call, the type, we go out hunting. Some of you all go to stupid, gullible

dating scenes like clubs, bars, church – yes church let's keep it real in

this book- and things of that nature. But you scoop the room out for

all those details and feelings that you've gathered that you are sure

will be the perfect match for you. You make eye contact, and you

find something that comes close to what your imagination decided.

You all go through the "get to know each other" stages, and the self-

evaluating goes into much more details and critical questions. Mixed

with your feelings, you are comparing and contrasting what your

goals were and what goals he/she doesn't commit to. Let's say the

date doesn't work out, which if you met him at a club, please don't be

surprised. You have to go back and reassess and do it again, and

again, then maybe another time, and maybe you think you got

it….then nope, not it again, then you try one more time, and that it

what you thought would be it. They are the one. They are perfect and

through all the ups and downs and roller coasters, honey you have

found the perfect one! That is how paying attention to detail should be, without the last part of going back and forth. That was very much

so exaggerated; however, I want you to look at this analogy.

Looking at yourself before the relationship, is looking at the event

and correctly accessing it and marking and feeling the foundation.

Everything Might Not Go As Planned! Things and humans will not

always operate as you want them to. How you adjust and maneuver

around the floor is your test of expertise at each event. Planning is

the number one way to eliminate any fears of last minute

adjustments. As you've made your budget, the miscellaneous amount

for each department is important. That amount should be 20-30% of

each department's total budget. Gives you room to breathe. Now that

the budget is somewhat covered finding a sponsor in that department

helps a lot. When two brands are both working towards a common

goal, their downfall is highly unlikely. When choosing your sponsors

make sure their mission is somewhat the same as yours. Nothing can ruin an event more than having a BBQ food sponsor at a Grand Gala.

Just thinking about it makes me think of messy. Even when linking

with sponsors double check that, the right equipment is in place for

the event. I like to think of an incident when I just knew everything

would go perfectly with my sponsor. I was an assistant coordinator

of an event I was working on with at the radio station. We were

launching our live broadcast out of Atlanta for the first time. So of

course, we went all out. Held the event at Patchwerk Studios. For

those who are unfamiliar with Patchwerk Studios, it's the biggest

studio in Atlanta. Greats such as 2 Pac, Biggie, Whitney Houston,

Lil Wayne, Young Jeezy, Pink, Destiny Childs and more have laid

tracks down in those walls. It was a complete honor to walk through

and see all those plaques. Anywho, as our liquor sponsor, we had

Seagrams gin. Now, this was so last minute; however, everything

and anything is possible with an amazing team comes together.

Everything was set perfectly as we awaited the arrival. They showed

up, thank heavens, however, the bar that they had, was NOT able to get inside the building. If anyone in branding knows, that the bar is their biggest promotion tool. Has big as day, Seagrams Gin with their logo on the front. At the moment, I'm thinking hard because in contracts with sponsors for events, giving that sponsor as much brand awareness as possible is KEY. Remember always to allow speakers to show gratitude to your sponsors throughout the event. Assure their brand logos are present and visual as possible. The studio is made with so many different twists and turns and angles, oh and SMALL DOORS. The bar had to get up the steps, which didn't work, then it had to get through the side door, that didn't work. Eventually, I pleaded with the Seagrams representative to allow us just to use a regular table. I asked, did he have a squirt, with their logo on it? He automatically remembered. That fact that I am aware of options makes the situation much better. And that's the key to always remaining above situations when everything doesn't go your way. Besides remaining calm, always look at the requirements, and look at the alternatives of each before the event. Honoring your contract is your word of YOUR brand, and in this career, your word

is everything. It's your fact and your representation. So represent

your brand correctly.

Chapter 4- Personally

Learn the art of your presence.

I have become so confident and in tune with myself that it sometimes scares me. Was that to honest? No. Learn to admit to yourself and who you are right now. Many insecure individuals are scared to work with an individual that is so confident. How you are feeling at this moment. Every emotion is removable. Go into all your doubts without fear, embrace, and let go. Start off every idea fresh. This is done effortlessly when always remaining at peace. This chapter is dedicated to the person that you are, during your career. Learn how to create the event, and not allow it to create you. If you think that's cliché, then you're not applying it to the capacity, and you're probably in denial. Which is alright, but you have to grow and learn your presence, quickly.

So when starting your entrepreneur journey, you want to have a clear

blueprint of where you are going. Do not go into this blind. No one

is perfect, and EVERYONE had a plan. Everyone's methods will not

be the same! When I was in Atlanta, I visited the African American

Museum, and in the Martin Luther King Jr. room there laid the most

amazing pieces of history I have ever seen. Handcrafted plans and

goals of Dr. King. His days, meetings, speeches and more were all

first written on paper. The ink and paper are POWERFUL things.

Never underestimate it. Never. Another misconception about our job

is how lucky we are to work with celebrities and famous people, and

this is true most, or at least some, of the time. It is great to truly

appreciate how someone has deservingly got where they are through

talent and charisma and seemingly managed to stay grounded.

HOWEVER, I think every #eventprof has horror stories of

egotistical, downright rude and dislikeable characters we have had

the "pleasure" to work with. But of course what happens backstage,

stays backstage – or at least until I write my memoirs!

Ladies and Gentlemen close your eyes and hug yourself for 30 seconds. Feel your arms, legs, hair, feet, and everything. Go ahead, see you in about thirty minutes.

Oh hey! How did it go? This is your temple. This is your powerful tool to create memories and dreams for millions. Understand that? One has to take care of that. The life we live can sometimes can a little unmanageable to have good exercise routines and diets. That's what someone with excuses would say, but we make time for what's most important to us. And this is the most important. After all the coffees and energy drinks we have to come back to the realization that we need the real nutrients. I know that with all the food we feel like Saturday morning at Sams Club! We get to bite and munch on everything, taste testing on the best dishes! However just as we plan events, we have to plan what we will eat daily. Following a strict regimen is key. Start to record the times that you are most hungry.

Our minds run off the food we consume, so we want to make sure that we are feeding our mind with the nutrients you deserve. The day before a busy event day or meeting day does it matter in this industry really; we need to plan each meal. Try to incorporate the restaurant's menu before going by looking via the website or your memory; because I'm sure this your favorite restaurant with the fried calamari that you love. Okay so back to your diet. Record your breakfast, snack, lunch, mid-snack, and dinner. This all should be prepared in a cute Louis book bag; speaking it into existence. The food you eat and the amount of activity your body goes through affects a lot. Eating more fruits, vegetables, whole grains, less red meats, fatty dairy products, and food that's overall high in calories and sugar, for a better temple. Exercising is something that we all daydream about right. Yes, and that's probably it, daydream. We have to be as active in the event space as we are on the field ladies and gentlemen. Running is the first start, a beautiful power run can start the mind of the right now. Workouts when you first wake up and before you go to bed helps release tension and any pulled up worries or concerns.

During my morning exercises, I pray through each crunch and push

up. The energy that you push into the atmosphere is glorifying. The

atmosphere brings into your world what your energy pushes, and if

you use aggression and enthusiasm into your prayers watch the

turnaround! Use your exercise as a way to become closer to your

true definition and purpose. Look at the positive results you will

receive.

Remember that everyone is going to make mistakes, but this is your

journey. Remain this as personal as possible. Share your vision,

however, don't share your plans with friends or family. Execute it

and state your testimony after. Let your work tell your story. Your

mistakes are yours because you need them. They are there to bring

you into a better understanding of what you will embark in the

future. Not only will you need them however you will be thankful.

Take your time and research, then develop what and who you really want to be. It's okay to say no sometimes. Make sure that you are comfortable and happy with what you are going further with. Sometimes in events, we have this "Yes Man" syndrome, but we got to kick it. I understand we have a lot going on and we have to focus.

Our decisions affect everything and everyone around us. Unfortunately, our decisions are not so sweet. We have to take into consideration the client and attendees. Our future and past clients. When making decisions, you literally have one second to decide yes or no based on the facts that are presently presented. But your happiness is key and final. That's what you have to wake up to and go to sleep too. No one can stop you from making decisions for yourself. Remember your time, your inner peace.

Chapter 5 -The Blueprint

I am about to share with you the blueprint for developing a

successful company. KEEP UP!

Lay your foundation by creating a wish list. You will soon turn that

into your BUSINESS PLAN! =) Make goals but make sure they are

smart. Draft your plans up. Have ideas of contacts, destinations, and

dates. Develop your start-up budget. Be smart, and save. Understand

that this is not the time to waste money. It is investing time. Start

building your wish list. Don't worry everything that is on that paper

will manifest with your hard work, consistency, and dedication. You

already have the love for it. Make sure you are thankful each and

every second of it. The energy you have when writing down your

goals has an impacting feeling. It is the journey that is the calm

before the storm. Make sure you are making adjustments along the way. Create assessments weekly, and always keep track of all your funds. Receipts, cash book, and file folders. When working from home, you have to be disciplined. Stay away from distractions like TV, phone, and social media. Try to meet clients at coffee shops, venue main offices or restaurants. Always have a backup plan for your meetings though like the library or your friend's apartment office space. Hiring a personal assistant or going solo is a choice that has to be well thought out as well. Go over your budget and see if you can hire an intern for school credit. That's your best bet. Always think about outsourcing before anything. Independent contractors, or partnering up with other companies. Get a few amazing mentors. People that will be completely dedicated to your success just as you are. Very honest and well-seasoned into the industry. Make sure you get a bank account with a bank that has great rates for businesses, for credit cards and loans for the future. Research a few lawyers regarding business ventures. Get a few quotes and do your research, research, research! Make sure that you both sign contracts on your part, confidentiality agreements, money security, and overall trust agreement. You may do your own research in that field, but just make sure this lawyer has your best interest in your company. When starting, keep track of your profit. Ensure you are progressing and taking your time. Forecast your revenue goals and start-up costs. Budget accordingly. Make sure you are taking into consideration all hicks up! What did I tell you about that? Hmmm. Determine your hourly billing rates or your packages. Most hourly rates are determined by the budget of the client and your overall skill and proficiency in the field. Packages are decided upon what you offer, and what you offer, is actually worth. Don't overdo yourself. Most clients can smell a rat. Don't be the rat, be the Lion. Just make sure you're doing your math for what will benefit you more. I would say ask a fellow event planner with their own event company that's been sufficiently running for at least 10 plus years. Invoice your clients on the regular and keep track of them all! Keeping track of them on an excel sheet or inputting them into a system. Pay vendors as soon as possible. Do not ever take their payments loosely. Working for a company that was always so behind on their payments on their vendor payments gave me so much clarity. Pay them always and get it out of the way. Their partnership is very important. I'll share a great story. I had just started working for the hotel management company. My boss at the time was training me on payments. He says, "Okay, so now I'm going to show you where the checks are." Thinking to myself, why would checks be sitting around. Doesn't sound right to me. But I followed, there were 6-7 bins with stacks of checks with over hundreds of thousands of dollars worth of checks for vendors. I was worried, like how can they pay me, if they owe all these vendors. SD: I'm always thinking of me. But anywho, he goes to show me how to pull checks that certain general manager's request. I immediately thought, if I were a vendor, I would come get my checks. Not like headquarters was in a secret location. As time went out, I followed procedures with pulling checks. One day I get a phone call from a general manager, she states "Hey so remember that check I asked you to send, the vendor is here cursing me out and

threatening me, can you please send this payment?" I saw that the

check was actually not pulled at all; however, I went ahead and took

care of it. What that made me wonder was, what if that individual

was hurt. That's the company's fault. And how could the company be

so selfish and naïve and do I want to work for a company that's this

careless? Not at all! When handling vendors, you assure the comfort

for not only yourself and business, but more importantly your staff.

The individuals that are handling your day to day tasks for your

baby. Taking care of them means that they will take care of you.

That brings me to the next big decision, which is getting a great

lawyer. Now that everything is on paper, your blueprint is doing,

everything should be mapped out. Business plan is complete, future

vendor contracts, sponsorship, and partnership contracts etc. has

been taken care of. You want to get a great business lawyer to advise

you on a lot of the future decisions you make. This goes with

controlling your revenue, making decisions and dealing with future partnerships. This is for you to look after you and your baby. As far as bank accounts, I do not suggest taking a loan for a business of such; however, it's your own choice. I will say, the best money that you put into your company will be your money. You feel more proud of yourself and your brand when this is being accomplished. Now you want to invest in an amazing financial management plan.

Read as many books as possible, seek as much advice, attend seminars/workshops and revise revise revise! Now when can you splurge? You're like, "NIA I WORKED SO HARD I'VE MADE THOUSANDS WHEN CAN I START SPENDING?!" I can't give you that book correct answer. I know that you should be working fully into your purpose for a year before you start using profit. Due to the many expense of starting a company. Starting off, everything that you take out, you put back double. I've used this technique with everything I've ever needed to save money, and it's an amazing habit. Most entrepreneurs knows it takes two to three years to start seeing a true profit from all your investing. However, you shouldn't be spending like crazy upon starting your company, ALL your profits should be saved. Prepare yourself for tax time! I would say speak to an accountant or financial consultant upon beginning your company.

Now I wouldn't be a real woman if I told you to work hard and never treat yourself! Spa days are so important! We are always running around like a crazy woman, remember always to keep your balance. Have faith, and you will soon realize that your hard work is true to pay off for itself. So don't rush it, don't push it, just relax. Sometimes I would work myself to death because I thought I wouldn't have any extra second tomorrow. I worked like it was my last second and minute. I spent all my money on my hustle and my grind. I had people raving about me left and right with no money in my pockets.

I just wasn't truly happy, happy for my success but not happy about my energy levels. It even had me questioning did I want this lifestyle. It took me so long to realize that I have to release. Now just use the moments with friends and family, but use time alone to become at total peace with myself and everything around me. When we have built up the tension, we tend to cause confusion and tension around us. When coming into this field, we need to realize the power our mindset has on the mood of the event and the entire situation. Becoming at peace allows your mind to be clear when making decisions. Having open minds allows us to make those quick decisions.

CHAPTER 6 #Eventproof?

Do you have what it takes? Are you ready? Now that you've seen the beginning of the wave, are you ready to ride it? Can you feel the success coming? Have you mastered separating professionalism and personal life? At the end, it comes down to your morals, what you feel is right and wrong. What you believe in your personal life, will not always adhere to your profession. You can't always mix the two because the two atmospheres will not always be acceptant of one another. Have a clear understanding of your personal ethics and your professional ethics. Personal ethics and ones that your personal value and qualities come from. Your professional ethics and ruled by the rules and regulations. The personal ethics you have are incorporated through memories, professional ethics are gathered by what you learn from your teammates, staff, and clients. With your personal lives, you have to be loving, caring and sincere. Assure in your profession that you have perfect time management, not gossiping and full confidence. In one instance you have to worry about disappointing others, in your work you're making sure reputation isn't destroyed. However, both needs are met, as long as you stand by what's right.

Now by this time you are the most organized bean in the world. I hope. I hope by this time you are almost fully #EventProof. I can't stress the level of importance organization is. It is what prepares you for your future blessings. Wait, read that sentence again. You can't leave any room for error. Crossing your teas and dotting your eyes will make sure that when your client comes they are speechless. Absolutely speechless. Great systems like podio.com, basecamp.com, and workboard.com are all great team communication sites to make sure the whole team is in one accord.

But I'm going to give you a great breakdown that will certify you #EventProof!

Create folders for your clients and vendors and create subfolders throughout. Certain subfolders should be labeled. I like to use Google Drive.:

- Client Folders

- Contacts

- Contracts

- Event Surveys

- Event Inquiry Application

- Employee/Volunteer folders

- Business (Tax ID, LLC, etc.)

- Professional Photos of Yourself and Team

- Vendor Folders

- Décor

- music

- entertainment

- photos

- rentals

- venues

Nothing is better than OLD FASHION. Once you've digitally gotten

yourself together let's take it old school. Get a huge binder 4'-5'

inch binder and create folders for each of the above bullet points.

Create a word document with a table and label the top with Name, Date, Address, Email, Social Media, Relationship, etc. If you believe in digital, then that's fine, I love google docs because I can get anything done ANYWHERE!

You should be updating your system and binder daily, weekly, monthly and yearly. But everyone once a week you should be cleaning out, keeping up and adding whatever is necessary.

Your relationship with your vendors must be a strict system. Always keep stacks of thank you cards! That's so important. Everyone gets thank you cards, especially the people that gave you the hardest times. I once bought a stack of beautiful thank you cards for no reason at all. But little did I know the reason was coming. I started to get the urge to send it to everyone. Thank you cards are a great way to release. When I was leaving my full-time job, I could not stand the secretary. Shoot, the whole time that I worked there, I couldn't stand my secretary. But anyways, when I left I didn't want to hold any negative energy with anyone in the building. My last day I started to write on the thank you cards to all the people I shared great moments with. I wrote a note to the secretary and spilled my heart out to her. You know I never look back, but looking back she's never responded. However deep down I know the respect is there. When sending thank you letters, you've sealed the deal, and you have the upper hand in the end.

A very good idea is to also have surveys in your thank you cards. These surveys should be detailed for clients, vendors, and attendees. Before, during and after experiences should questions. Take this data and study it and analyze it personally and professionally.

Let's face it. If you are one of us event planners and wish to live a full life, you'll have to multitask. Here are three insights about multitasking in the context of how your brain works, and three tips that might help you be more effective at multitasking.

Three helpful tips I can give you that will help you better control multitasking:

1.Only multitask when it is really necessary. Micromanage.

2.Don't multitask in your relationships. Bring full presence at all times.

3. When the pressure is on DO NOT try to multitask. Focus.

Being #Eventproof means you're proficient at time management.

Being resistant will cause a lack in you work habits. Resistance is

when you feel as though you are forcefully doing something. Don't

feel compelled and do what you feel. As I've said before, you should

be controlling your feelings at all times. Just as you control your

mind, you can control your feelings. Feelings are just things that are

removable and placed wherever you think it's okay to stay. Learn the

art of not being resistant, and just do what you think about doing.

Get should or shouldn't out of your head, and do what you feel. If

you feel like making the to-do list, do it, and do not resist. Use that

amazing list that you've made for yourself and now, let's add due

dates to it. Give yourself a certain amount of hours, days, weeks and

sometimes months. Be realistic but don't resist your due dates. Stay

committed to yourself and your word. Most people that tell you what

you should do, you won't do. Why is that? Because no one likes to

be told what to do. Neither do you. So don't tell yourself to do

something, feel it, and then do it. Stop using multi-tasking as the only solution. As I've said above, learn when you should multi-task. It's not always needed. Micro-manage, the key to all success is something that you are literally doing both at the same time.

Working ahead is another way that multitasking and micromanaging can be easier. As I said stop being resistant. Whatever you think, do it, and don't think twice or procrastinate. Whenever you have thought that makes you resists, ask yourself, "Can I sacrifice this for my success?" "Will laying down help me accomplish my vision?" Your answer may be "No." Then you ask yourself, "So can I let go of this resistance to have the success I want?" Then I hope you would say "Yes." Now "Can you let go of it right now?" The key words, DON'T PROCRASTINATE. Usually, when you tell your mind not to do something, you're going to do. So whatever you think of doing, just do it, because you'll end up having a back and forth thing in your mind that wastes valuable work time. This goes for on the field and off. You never want to get behind on the chores because you've been working on projects all week. Take that 10-15 minutes that it takes to clean the bathroom a day, or kitchen. Whichever needs to be fixed. Drop that package off, on your way to the meeting. Maximize the 24 hours in a day that you have. This has a lot to do with waking up early in the morning. The early bird gets the worm first has to be the most cliché quote, however realistic as ever. As you will notice or should have, we get so much done when we wake up early enough. You can't make money while you sleep, and if you can, then you must already be making millions honey. What you need this book for? No, don't put the book down, can you keep on reading. Not only do you have to maximize your time, but you have to work expeditiously on tasks. This has to do with making smart decisions. Outsourcing properly, distributing tasks correctly and time management. Utilize your team. I've discussed how important giving certain people certain tasks.

Problem-solving. If you're going to be #EventProof you have to be a great problem solver. As I have said, some things may go wrong. Everything isn't going to work the way you want it to. Understanding that you can't change every situation will make you less stressed. When you think in your head, "I wish this could happen!" "I want this to go this way, " and you can't stop thinking about it, stop it. Just stop, calm down and ask yourself can I actually physically stop it or change it from happening? Do I really have some type of control over this? If the answer is no, ask yourself to let it go and move on. We have big fish to fry and dreams to help be produced to reality.

Crazy, sexy and cool. Okay, no that's TLC. Play it cool, calm and collective. Answers should always be monotone. Be cool; there is really nothing to stress over unless it has been a true life threating tragedy. Planning properly can help gain your cool. It will help everything collective. Can't nobody tell you nothing? Your client should enjoy every single life breathing second! Before, during and after. All their requests must be made – unless they just have an OBVIOUS TRAGIC BUDGET and them running on hopes and dreams and not Benjamin. The strength and success of an event are dependent on the event management's ability to integrate its many subparts. Major events need to be planned for long in advance, period. You may think they seem simple; locales need to begin to worry about everything from event customer service to event security. Event should be easy to interact in a seamless and in a precise manner. Our strengths are told in numbers. The most that you have at the end, the more you win. Is always the motive for me. Find ways to cut costs by researching travel patterns. Study the event participants' travel patterns, keep vehicles filled, work with local venues to find ways to cut costs, create ways for people to want to share in the event's costs through sponsorships, meet the celebrities or donations. Remember the more money that is collected, the less the public will need to pay, and the happier event attendees may be. Develop flexible timelines. No matter how well you plan, things will change over time. Service provider's change, people start new businesses, die or retire, and weather conditions may produce unforeseen delays. The trick is to practice the art of redundancy; have numerous backup plans and assume that most things will take about 20% longer to accomplish than first contemplated. Furthermore, many industries providing goods and services to an event may see "opportunistic costs." This means that they assume that they can jack up prices, as the event planner will have no alternative but to pay. To avoid these problems, attempt to secure multiple sources, purchase early and demand contracts that lock into service providers to a set price.

That brings me to budgeting. You're not #EventProof if you can't manage a budget properly. Doing little, but a lot, with a little is the key. Okay, I just confused myself. Individuals should be smart enough coming into this industry knowing that cutting cost as much as possible is important. We are aware that our main focus is satisfying our clients, but what about our partnerships. The key is you take care of your vendors. They are the ones that follow you throughout your career. They are the ones that offer referrals the most ironically. The secret of maintaining relationships is your self-control. Understand that everyone does not think like you and you are the one in charge of your destiny. Do not ever be upset about misfortunes that vendors get their selves into. You can change event situations. Except, weather, and that just means you've got a lot of making up to do. One of my culinary chefs from school always stated, it's not about your screw up, it's about your recovery. No one forgets your past mistakes, but everyone can respect you for how you handle and recover it. Your mission is to keep the client so in the clouds that all mistakes are invisible and impossible to them. I can't stress how important it is to remain great relationships with these vendors so that negotiating prices will be an ease. Stay in a positive mental attitude, smile and always refer them to your fellow career colleagues. You want the lowest prices on all things that are reoccurring in your events. I can give your great tips for maintaining a low budget.

When planning the full event out, you want to set high expectations for yourself. Create budgets that are so low and do your best to stand by them. Four main requirements you should set for yourself is 1) Budget 2) Event Date and Time 3) Head Count 4) Space Requirements. This is just to scratch the surface. Make sure you use all the evidence you can find. I know you've watched Snapped, Law&Order or CSI. We have to search deep. Interview all suspects, people close to the clients, our vendors and prospective attendees, which is mainly our target market. Bring all you got to the table when doing negotiations and sending over logistics and prospects to venue managers and vendors.

Secret: When calling vendors and venues that you are just using for the first time, never state your budget, state, "We are still working on the budget, can you just give me the best prices available?"

This method only works with companies you are using for the first time. But, they will be more than likely from there, give you the highest prices and you negotiation it down from there. GO!

Are you a realistic event planner. Can you predict well? How many people are you known for this client to bring? They say they will have hundreds of people. You know maybe fifty will show. A lower headcount makes for a lower cost for food, beverage and hotel rooms. You want to have a clear timeline so that you can use a less time a possible. Event times have changed so much now. Everything is a minimum amount of hours due to that first hour of no one really showing up. Know your target market! But don't just stop at one venue, do your research and spend a few days shopping to venues. Do not get caught up in sales talk. They will trick you in a minute just to distract you from a strict timeline that you have to adhere to. When you look for venues though, really look. I know hotels are so easy, but get creative. Use art museums, boutique shops, and single venues. Believe it or not, food cost at hotels are much higher. The outside research on caters and ancillary costs may be time-consuming but its well worth it. And you gain new relationships that have the opportunity to turn into partnerships. Have multiple dates that they can work with you on. If this is a venue that you've done your research and seen that, they don't get booked that often, then don't take that route. But if this is a venue with high traffic, try to book future events with them as well before your initial event. Now, say you've chosen the venue, and everything is rocking and rolling.

Treat everyone you cross paths with, with ultimate respect. These

will be the ones that you have long-term partnerships with. Staff and

managers should know you by the first name and to always be

pleasant. Book future events with them as well. Do not demand

ridiculous things, and try to remain as independent as possible

regardless. But micromanage, there's that word again, wisely. Treat

them as you would want to be treated. Have your logistics for done

perfectly. Therefore, the staff at the venues know what you cannot

do, and what they need to accommodate with and likewise for both

parties. Always place your staff in proper places, before the venue

staff. That's a great secret. Look at the goals of venues, to keep it

packed every day and to gain the highest cost of every event. Show

that you value them, just as you value your companies. Consider

supply versus demand, and look at the venues that are more likely to

be booked and which are not. Some are high, just because they are

receiving that high traffic already. Some need it so that they will give you the best price. You want to go for the venues that need the exposure, and take the challenge to bring it the most revenue. Look at the time of the year that the venue is in demands. Try to book around the days of the week that they are less likely to be fully booked with a high event cost. For example, you're more likely to get a good price for meetings on the weekends and weddings on weeknight weekends such as Friday or Sunday. Those are just some of the secrets. As you grow, you will learn more.

So are you #Eventproof?

Part II

Chapter 5 – The Marketing Bean

A wise woman once told me, for you to be a successful event planner you have to be willing to promote your ASS off. Sorry for all the church people reading this right now. But I'm going to keep it real with you at all times. You have to understand that in this day and age our events have different aspects of marketing now. Print marketing, social media marketing, email marketing and direct marketing. Now I will break all of these down, but of course, I want to break down the main fundamentals of mental marketing. Napoleon Hill once taught fundamentals of marketing through the mental capacity in which we use every day. He showed the world just how changing our minds can change the amount of money in our pockets. He changed my life forever reading his books. It all started when I first read the book, "The Secret" by Rhonda Byrne. I wanted

to know where she got such knowledge from. I've always been like

that, wondering why things happened, and digging deeper. I started

looking at the authors and speakers of the quotes that she had

throughout the book. I began researching them and reading their

books. I stumbled on napoleon hill and understood where it all came

from. I found these 13 principles in his "Think and Grow Rich

Book." Definiteness of Purpose, The mastermind alliance, going the

extra mile, applying faith, have a pleasing personality, self-

discipline, positive mental attitude, enthusiasm, personal initiative,

overcoming adversity, creative vision, accurate thinking and the law

of attraction. From these principles, I learned to be a marketer. It

didn't just come to me, however, by performing these acts the

knowledge came to me. Go do your research and come back to me!

Now I can go on days and days about the principles however I want to show you how they each relate to events. The mastermind alliance is number one in marketing your events. The relationships that you build, especially in your community, will follow you. You want to make sure you have alliances in every department of events. Venues, food and beverages, décor and more. This will eliminate constant negotiations. Designed templates that will be easy for you and your "partner" agreements. This agreement will be the defendant goal that you both want to obtain for one another. Something that will be easy to change the numbers. A strategic alliance can be defined as two or more organizations working together towards a common goal without money changing hands. Highlighted benefits of forming alliances with your peers; Share the cost. Share the cost of the venue, marketing, registration, etc. Do not be afraid to partner up with organizations like yours. Think how much you could cut on cost? Some other companies have more expertise in areas that you do not. You can leverage from that by doubling your profit, attendees, new partners, new knowledge, and more. This is not only a networking opportunity for you, however, also for your attendees. Know-a-days events are made to socialize more rather than just party. However, understand your target market. I'll dig even deeper, look at the economy pricing. When you purchase more, you get it for cheaper. With a high guest count, you will need more food, more rooms, more employees, etc. Your ROI will skyrocket. Partnerships gain more exposure and a high budget. Therefore you can purchase celebrity appearances and performances, better décor, and more.

Build that network!

Going the extra mile is one of the most important things that you can take from this book. This is your formula for constant blessings. We are blessed negotiators and so creative; however, we must remain that business mindset, which is remaining two steps ahead at all times in all areas. The growth of knowledge builds your longevity in this industry. Let me give you the secrets for going the extra mile in events. By keeping an open mind and eyes, you learn so much. Always have the humble heart with a willingness to learn. Success will be effortless to come to you. Do not be stubborn, learn to do things differently. Use those apps, stop being old school, use what will work best and quick. Always jump out there and learn as much as possible about your clients and their ideas. Take that extra mile and change your researching skills, change the scenery of where you usually market. There's no such thing as useless information, so wear as many different hats as possible. Learn job descriptions of all your employees and vendors. Always go the extra mile by planning for safety. Think about safety routes and drills. Have a standard format, however, a great tool to have in your bag.

Remaining in faith. I can sum up faith into your whole life, but I will break it down for you. Faith is about fighting from the beginning till the end, and your passion fuels you. You have to understand and let go of fear. Controlling your faith has a lot to do with controlling your emotions. As the pastor always says, "Faith without works is dead" You have to go that extra mile and take a leap of faith and believe that you can achieve any and everything you believe in. When planning events, the number one thing that will make you successful is faith in your client. You have to believe that nothing will come your way that you are not built to handle, and with a PLAN- and we ARE event PLANners- you can do some pretty amazing things. Have faith in yourself. Have just as much faith in your planning. Erase your fears, and be bold! Try that new pattern, try that new vendor and just explore creativity. Remember that feeling/emotions are things, and it's totally in your control and can be easily removed. So remove it.

Remain a pleasing personality. While I'm telling you how it's going to explain the why. Always smiling and remaining cheerful has gotten me almost everything that I want. I have stories for days about how I smiled and batted my eyelashes, and then I simply had exactly what I needed in my hands. This goes for the big things too. Every moment that you feel you are in complete control, you will get a test. A test from the higher power that will only make you better.

So don't feed into the negativity, it's here to make you stronger. Always open yourself and allow your skills and talent to flourish! Be flexible and allow yourself to adapt to change swiftly. Always have a purpose and stay true to it. Don't spend long on decisions, take the chance, and have faith. So don't hesitate, when you want to speak, speak. Thinking long on decisions can literally block blessings; you have to keep your mind at peace and open. Have courtesy and always respect other people feelings. I believe in treating others how you want to be treated because you should always treat yourself with courtesy and love. Tact is knowing what and how to say when to say it. Everything is not for everyone ears. Always keep your voice

monotone. Always keep a smile on your face. Never allow someone

to take it off. Keep it. Matter of fact. Smile right now. And every

time you pick this book up, smile, smile while you are reading. Keep

smiling! Honestly, direct your feelings to a state of being genuine,

and smile. Your facial expression should always remain just as

genuine as your smile. As I said adapting quickly will allow you to

learn how to deal with others emotions and actions better. Learn that

others decisions do not dictate your feelings. The more intolerant

you are, the more closed off to the diversity of the world and the

power of the spiritual side of the mind. Have a frankness when you

speak to people and keep that habit for every person that you meet.

Don't give that habit up; it will make you stand out against your

peers. I know some of us aren't the funniest in the world, but we

have to learn how to make people laugh. Make people feel good

around you. Faith is woven into every principle of the philosophy of

achievement; faith is the essence of great achievement, no matter what its nature or purpose. Neglecting your faith while carrying your

definite major purpose would be like trying to study astronomy

without referring to the stars. It's always great to take a speech class

or two, and even three. How you cultivate your words will make for

a clear understanding. The most important thing to do when

remaining a pleasing personality, have complete emotional control. I

know that event planning is our thing, I know, trust me, but you can't

stop educating yourself. Take as many classes as you can year

around. Always remain a student to life. Our clients come from all

types of areas, and you want to make sure that you can relate to each

part. So you must swallow that pride, and take away all the arrogant

natures. ALWAYS keep your eye on YOUR prize. Remain focused,

and don't stand around gossip, and playing around. Time is money,

and life, those are two things you cannot spare to lose. So always

congratulate your peers, and when people are doing well, tell them.

Seal the deal with two final things, a nice firm handshake, and

personal magnetism. You should channel this energy into your efforts making them, not your body, the source of appeal to others.

Use your sexual energy to build your enthusiasm, to display your

genuine fondness for people, to burnish your style and tone of voice.

Your gesture and posture too will reflect this quality.

Self-discipline. This here is another ultimate secret. Something that

many take for granted. Don't be quick to check others but can't check

yourself. With self-discipline, you are gaining so many new skills,

knowledge and overall ability to live a better life. And plan events

better also. Learning ways to control your self-discipline is not

simple. But it's for the strong-minded. I can truly say that you will

not be successful without this. I'll give you give easy controlled

mechanisms. First one is; avoid temptations. You cannot be around

what you know triggers you; you have to know yourself. Sit down

and access your pet peeves and stay away from those environments

that you think would be around it. Having a healthy diet is just as important as well. You know what happened to the Cookie Monster

when he didn't get any cookies? The same applies to the human

world. Food and beverages have a lot to do with our emotions.

Feeding the brain keeps the energy flowing and ideas pouring. We

need that! It's our secret weapon. Do not crunch all those hours

without at least two meals, water, and some exercise. Number 3,

don't wait on anything. Part is discipline is change, and that can get

uncomfortable. That's good, don't be afraid. Go through with your

head held high and your faith even higher. Learn how to embrace

your mistakes. Number four, don't be so hard on yourself baby. Give

yourself breaks, pace yourself and reward yourself. You have to take

it back to grade school. Reward yourself after a hard five or six

hours or research and preparation. That's an example. But this is a

hard task, so you deserve to reward yourself. But be honest with

yourself and know your limits. Last but not least, forgive yourself.

Forgive all those that did you wrong, or you feel was wrong also.

When you fail, forgive yourself and move right along. No one is perfect and remembers the rule before that; you have to know and yourself.

Enthusiasm! Say it again, but with excitement. Feel that? Feel that tingle inside of you? Kind of how you get when you're reading this book! All your feelings and thoughts should be filled with enthusiasm about your task. Those tingles inside create an amazing transfer of energy into the universe that draws your desires closer to you. Don't underestimate it. Always make sure you laugh and smile. All your answers should end with complete grace and excitement. Some people say, "Oh I have bad days, I can't be excited all the time." Lies. You never let your bad days show. Your passion is what is going to make you shine. Few tips on how to remain enthusiastic about life and your work. This quote from American businessman Edward B. Butler (1853-1928) ties into Bettger's advice:

"Every man is enthusiastic at times. One man has enthusiasm for 30 minutes – another for 30 days, but it is the man who has it for 30 years that makes a success out of his life."

To be enthusiastic, you have to ACT more enthusiastic. You are the master of your mind; you have full control of your future actions. Wake up daily and state, I am enthusiastic about my day, my life and the future. I am powerful. Second, Draw strength from the positive. Think about times that you were your most happiest. Use that feeling you get during that imagery and use it for all current moments. Step three, always record your "aha" moments. That's what Oprah calls them. They are those ideas that pop up in your mind while you're busy. You have to stick to that thought, repeat three times and confirm you have memorized it. The first free moment you get, go write it down in your handy journal or the notes on your phone. Refer to those notes all the time, and plan to execute them. As event planners sometimes are "Aha" moments are during the preparation of the event. Event set-up, or something while you're already crazy busy. Go with that feeling, of course, analyze it, and then execute it. Risk always brings us great blessings. Step four; don't dwell on the negative – Don't think about past mistakes. Put them out of your mind. And stop worrying about things you can't change. That's a definite. Step five; make a list of things that you are grateful for. And every time you feel yourself being less enthusiastic, think of that moment in your life that you were most joyful for. Step six, always be upfront and identify with what is holding you back. The best method that I have ever read was the Sedona Method. I was in total love with that book, and I still am. It helped me get over the most depressing things in my life. I want you to order that book. It's worth it, or even go to YouTube and watch the video. Ask yourself, do you accept what is holding you back? Can you let what is holding you back go? When can you let it go? Now? Great do so now. Last, step seven, don't listen to the negative. Let the pessimistic individuals stay where they are, and you keep moving forward. The

insecure has a funny way of trying to make you feel bad. Don't let it

control you.

Personal initiative. Researchers have found that successful people

take the initiative more. That's a no-brainer. How successful do you

want to be and how bad do you want it? How far are you going to go

to get it? What walls are you going to break down to see it happen?

Because there will be walls, aka tests, and you have to attack them

correctly. The personal initiative I found is critical to your progress

and sustainability. This is what makes you stand apart from the

different event planners. What you take from this industry will give

you the respect you deserve. When taking the initiative, these are the

ways that one must condition their mind. Always look for something

that you can make work better. And when you do so make sure you

come with a full plan and layout. Give it away or take charge and make it happen! Be the first at new ideas and policies. Be the example. Always look at different ways on how you can save money. Make sure you are always cost-efficient. Reach out to your teammates and assure that they are doing fine. Their progress is your progress. Volunteer and take on the toughest tasks. Always, always, always think ahead. Your plans should be well thought out that have backup plans. Prepare answers to questions that may be asked. Always look at your work from another eye. The eyes of the individuals that will be seeing your work. Research, research, research! Deal with problems immediately, don't wait long and handle them correctly. Lastly, always accept pure responsibility for your life. For your actions and mistakes. I would recommend Kaizen Journal for more tips. This is a trait that has to be disciplined.

Overcoming adversity. When overcoming adversity, you have to overcome your fears. As it says, OVERCOMING, this is for the equipped and strong. Know that once entered into the world of event planning you will no doubt be faced with adversity. Just think of a time where you wanted to really succeed at something, of course, there were changes in the initial plans. What's most important, did you give up? I hope not because being #Eventproof doesn't include that feature. Building that confidence of being able to overcome adversity comes from your initial entrance into the industry. Your relationships and confidence that you make in the beginning will make you solid. One of my greatest mentors told me that it's the confidence that you have when you walk in the room. You have to act like you're supposed to be there. The start of a relationship and the ending is crucial. Burning bridges are the first thing that will end your career pretty quickly. This is an industry of critical thinking when it comes to your actions and statements. When the two things are solid, overcoming adversity should be simplistic. You and

humans are the key to the universe.

These are steps that I've taken are have been told to take to overcome

adversity. Allow yourself to write all your goals down. Your goals

about finances, friend and love relationship and more. Take that goal

and break it down it 4 quarters of the year. Then take that list and

break it down into another two months, and that should be fine,

however, if you want to get in more detail then break it down into 30

days. This is simple, take your goals, and figure out what you need

to make your goals a success. Take that needed list and break it

down. Next, now that you have that list look around at your peers

and surroundings. You will start seeing the universe connect your

goals soon. After, ask questions, as much as possible. No questions

are dumb questions, so you might as well ask the questions. One that

doesn't ask will not get further. I've gained great friendships from attending events and conferences and just looking over to my right or left to ask my peers a question. And another after that, don't hesitate, even the ones that respond with an attitude. At least you have the upper hand in the room, you know who's grumpy and not to be bothered.

Creative vision. "When your Daemon is in charge, do not try to think consciously. Drift, wait, and obey." — Rudyard Kipling. When maintaining a creative vision, you have to have three strong qualities. Peace, patience, and initiative. We are all creative. Do not read this and think I will magically make you creative, because honestly, you are already creative. You have to understand how to master your mind and tell it what to do. Exercise that. There's no exact time when creativity starts, and it's terrible to try to control it. The most important thing you can remember to do when being creative as an event planner is to assure you are targeting all five senses. The guest should feel like they have an emotional connection with the event. This begins all the way from the title. Elements that should include a lot of creativity are the title, invitations, venue, catering, lighting, seating, design props, staff, stage, table linens, chairs, entertainment and more. Another strong creativity element is another human. Two heads are very much so better than one. Don't be afraid to partner up with colleagues, businesses, and vendors that specialize in being creative until you understand how to use the skill.

Yes, in my opinion being creative is a skill.

Accurate thinking. Accurate thinking is key when developing your marketing strategy. Knowing your target market is key to being #Eventproof. Now their types of accurate thinking, flexible and accurate. As event planners, we have to do both. We have to be

resilient and have the decisions before anyone can see the problem.
Being a flexible thinking event planner requires an ability to listen to
other people's opinions, have multiple solutions to a problem, and
having a Plan B is a core component in flexible thinking. To be
resilient requires flexible and accurate thinking, seeing different
perspectives. Someone who is resilient can come up with a variety of
reasons for being successful in something. Flexible and accurate
thinking allows multiple solutions to a problem, having Plan B and C
is vital to resilience.

And the law of attraction. Here now we come to an end, and
honestly the most important. Everything you just read leads up to the
law of attraction. Accurate thinking, positive mindset, creative
vision, they all have to do with the law of attraction. Marketing is all
MIND. These steps have never let me down. When meeting with any
person in the industry, think of it as a chance for you to promote

your company, even if it's done subtly. You can easily accomplish

marketing yourself as an event planner by making sure you hand out

your business card wherever you see fit, mentioning your company

or services wherever you can, and making sure the guests at each

event you created know where to contact you for future contracts.

Put your goals in the world, and they will sure manifest back into

your hands. Law of attraction is something that I hold so dear to me

because I've fallen victim to negative thinking. You live off of your

thoughts, and whatever you think will manifest. The last few

paragraphs set your mind up for a healthy thinking pattern. The cells

in your body grow off the emotions that your subconscious dictates.

So it is your job to keep your conscious socially aware of the things

that you desire to manifest. No aspect of your life is not affected by

your thoughts.

Chapter 9 - The Tech Bean

Social media is an important marketing component. Nothing is like gorilla market, good old face to face marketing. But this day and age social media is impactful. I don't want you to get blinded by just social media though, apps, text alerts and all are the components to assure that you are above your competition. Please believe that these things take real investments. Earlier I mentioned in the book how you should not be spending any profit, for it is important that you are locking down expenses. The expenses being paid is important when you want to market for your clients properly. Not all events are going to come, ALREADY PUT TOGETHER. These things take work, day in and day out, around the clock. Marketing moments come in all shapes and sizes. Utilize technology to your advantage to ensure continued growth in such an innovative society.

Taking it one step at a time. As I've previously described in this book, having a plan is key. Know what kind of results that you want to generate from social media, and plan how to get those results. Take your time to get to know your client, viewing their current social media, knowing they're real-life actions and sit them down and really get to know them as a human being. Ask them about their wants and needs, when you see what they aspire for, portray that over time in your posts.

Make it personal, but not too personal. You want your event to be engaging, have them talking, before, during and after. Keep to make it personal, know what triggers your target and deliver it effortlessly and unnoticeable. Each day your content should be delivering something different, getting in tune with another emotion. A video, a picture, funny memes, quotes, boomerangs and more. The world of content could go as far as a blank, white screen. Leave the post filled with curiosity, and you've won your attendee over. Now, don't go confusing that attendees with difficult insider jokes, take your time and see what they are already laughing and posting at. While creating the post for our company launch event, we made sure that the post was something that we know that our industry would like. Posted videos of people from the community, posted motivational quotes that we knew our peers could relate to, due to past stories. All times, are marketing moments. I hate to say this, but when people are the most vulnerable, that release their secret spots. Attackkkkkkk on the secret spots. They are YOUR best friend. Get personal.

Listen to feedback. Technology has granted us so much access to individual's lives. It's so easy to listen and read opinions nowadays. Things such as event apps, event systems, and Google help us remain contact with attendees. The most important part of marketing is the end of the end. The results are important tools for your next events. What you do with the attendee's information is important, you must organize them, follow up with thank you's and ask for event opinions.

Use as many platforms as possible in different ways. Each platform is targeted for a different market. This goes along with your market research, learning what your attendees use. Upon realization of the event theme, one can already depict the crowd. From there you should be pushing your marketing strategies to their liking. I'm not going to say that it will be easy. This takes a lot of research, time, gas, food, money, lunch/brunch/dinner dates, phone conversations, newspapers, books, magazines and more! Then take all that research and put it back into your marketing tools. Make sure that you hear their wants and needs the most. Solve the problem, before it starts, and you will be seen as the hero.

Conclusion

So now I ask, can you be #Eventproof? I never wrote this book with a mission to tell you what to do, but how you should feel. Feel the acceptance of your blessings. Know that without a doubt you've been brought to this world to create memories and experiences. Unforgettable ones. No one said that you would have all the answers, and sometimes, no all the time, it's not going to go how you want it. Giving up is not an option and when you think, how could you give up on your dreams? Being #EventProof is for the event planners that are ready to give it your all. Willing to put in your blood, sweat, and tears into your clients and attendees wants and needs. Being that sacrifice. It's your passion that keeps you pushing through, and if you ever lose that, you lose everything. Peace and blessings.

NiaEvents

Tanzania Rice

Tanzania "NiaEvents" Rice was born in Silver, Spring Maryland. From a youth, she showed independence, drive, and ambition. Nia is an event planner, brand builder, publicist and author of event planner guide; "#EventProof". In high school, Nia had the pleasure of planning prom, homecoming socials, and other social events. Being apart of the dance team she experienced planning shows and competitions. Entering college she knew that Event Planning was her passion. At the University of Maryland Eastern Shore, she studied hospitality management and received her degree from the top program in the state of Maryland for hospitality. At UMES she interned for one of the top PR firms and event companies within the Washington D.C. area. Upon graduating she took a position at a former Sirus-XM radio station 66 Raw. There she went from interning to running events, marketing, becoming head of public relations and assisting the program director. After working with the company for a few years, she branched out with her then colleague, Megan Alston and they both founded Serene MGMT.

Serene MGMT is the all-inclusive branding private island. Serene MGMT specializes in events, public relations, marketing, social media, graphics and more. Opening in September 2016, Serene MGMT has worked with some of the top entertainment companies and brands on the east coast. This dynamic duo has since opened a location in not only Washington D.C., but also, New York and North Carolina. The brand has worked with; Atlantic Records International dancer and Ncredible recording artist Yvng Swag, International Records Artist Letoya Lucket, Clothing Brand; Shoe City, NonProfit- Toys for Tots, Author, Blogger and Fashion Mavin, Claire Slummers and more. The company has founded a nonprofit called, "Ladies in the Industry: Music and Media" where they execute two conferences and 4 brunches a year. LITI, as they call it, brings women together within the music and media industry to discuss facing adversities, build genuine bonds, and strengthing your "Lady Boss" network. Serene has no plans on stopping, they are constantly growing.